great burgers

MOUTHWATERING RECIPES

Bob Sloan

Photographs by Jonelle Weaver

CHRONICLE BOOKS

SAN FRANCISCO

Library of Congress Cataloging-in-Publication Data:
Sloan, Bob.
  Great burgers : Mouthwatering recipes /
by Bob Sloan ; photographs by Jonelle Weaver.
       p. cm.
ISBN 0-8118-4293-2 (hardcover)
1. Cookery (Beef) I. Title.
TX749.S54 2004
641.6'62—dc22
                    2003015015

Manufactured in China.
Design and typesetting by Carole Goodman,
  Blue Anchor Design
Food stylist: Liza Jernow
Assistant food stylist: Jennifer Cohen
Prop stylist: Paige Hicks
Photographer's assistant: Teresa Horgan

Photographer Jonelle Weaver wishes to give special
thanks to Paige Hicks, Liza Jernow, Jennifer Cohen, and
Teresa Horgan for long hours of work; Scott and Lisa
Isherwood, Kate Green, The Parker House Inn, and the
Quechee Lakes Landowners Association for lovely
locations; and Per Furmark for home base support.

Distributed in Canada by Raincoast Books
9050 Shaughnessy Street
Vancouver, British Columbia V6P 6E5

10 9 8 7 6 5 4 3 2

Chronicle Books LLC
85 Second Street
San Francisco, California 94105

www.chroniclebooks.com

Old Bay® is a registered trademark of Old Bay
Company.

ACKNOWLEDGMENTS

I'd first of all like to thank Leslie Jonath for thinking of me for this project and Laurel Mainard for all her support and hard work in helping the book come together. Less critical was the willingness of many friends to sample the burgers as I was testing the recipes (like that really was such a hardship): The Mintz/ Stewart clan, the Warner/Kamslers, Susie and Mario, Richard Botwin, Lloyd Lynford, Phil and Sally, and Effie. David Sanfield was his usual indispensable self, and Mario Batali gave me some helpful tips, several of which had to do with food. Of course, I would like to thank my family—Randi, Nate, and Leo—who ate burgers for two months straight without complaining, or at least never within earshot.

TABLE OF CONTENTS

INTRODUCTION

ABOUT THE BURGER

There are several charming stories about the birth of the burger. All of them are true. Or none. It hardly matters. Any story of the burger's origin does little to enhance what each of us knows empirically. At some time in our lives, after taking a bite of a juicy, perfectly cooked burger, we've said, either aloud or to ourselves, something to the effect of, "This burger is as good as anything I've ever tasted."

Its sublime simplicity makes the burger one of the elemental tastes—what other tastes are compared *to*. Burgers are also one of those foods for which we have almost wanton cravings, a kind of burger mania—*"I so feel like having a burger now"*—that unique confluence of longing and hunger whose locus is the burger. This is not the same as wanting to dine at a certain restaurant or thinking you should probably eat fish tonight. Burger lust is not casual, but a deeper, more visceral desire, like the need to play a quick nine holes or listen to some early Miles Davis.

The burger is working class, a solid citizen—a humble and unpretentious marriage of meat and heat. In an age of flash and Baroque excess, the burger maintains its Romanesque simplicity, understated, bold, and sturdy. Gussy up a burger too much and it looks out of place, like a farmer in a tux.

So then how come a cookbook with so many different burgers? Because as Mae West was wont to say, "You can never get too much of a good thing." These recipes find ways to enhance the essential burger, without seeking to replace it. Though they require more preparation than the basic burger's simple "shape and flip," they are not overly labor intensive. I would never be so brazen as to suggest you might tire of the basic burger, but rather that you may want to try exploiting the burger as a vehicle for some killer preparations that go beyond it.

COOKING

Burgers are forgiving. When the butcher grinds the meat, fat and muscle are so intertwined that the burger becomes self-basting. All you have to do is not overcook it. For me, the perfect burger is medium-rare. When sliced in half, it is a frame of charred meat surrounding a roseate middle section that at its center is a deep claret. Decide for yourself what the perfect burger is and try to cook it the same way each time. Figure on an extra minute for each increment, i.e., 9 minutes total cooking time for medium-rare, 10 minutes for medium, 11 minutes for medium-well. Of course, all stoves and pans differ slightly, and the heat on your charcoal grill will also vary, so stay attentive. You can always cut into one of the burgers to check for doneness. Eat that one yourself, or better yet, serve it to one of the kids.

Chicken, turkey, and pork burgers must be cooked all the way through, so remove them at the moment they are done to avoid overcooking. Again, if you have to slice into one to check, it's okay—it will be hidden soon enough under the condiments and bun.

SIZE

Is bigger better? Some aficionados covet burgers of monstrous proportions, like they are undertaking a week's worth of eating at one sitting. They seek out burgers that start out as a large mass of meat and end up, once cooked, resembling a softball hit out of the park one too many times. Following considerable testing for this book, 6 ounces of meat per burger was determined by young and old to be the perfect size for a burger. After cooking, it still has some heft, but it's not overblown—more like a linebacker than a defensive end. Smaller, thinner burgers usually wind up getting overcooked and merely serve to add but a hint of meat flavor to the bun and condiments. A 6-ounce burger also works well with the heat generated from a noncommercial home range.

PAN VS. GRILL

All of the recipes here were tested on a 12-inch cast-iron pan on a standard domestic gas stove. Many were also cooked on outdoor gas and charcoal grills. (I don't recommend using the broilers on most domestic stoves; their area of intense heat is too narrow to cook 4 burgers uniformly.) There was no appreciable difference in taste, and cooking time is pretty much the same: a 6-ounce beef burger takes about 9 minutes total to cook to medium-rare on a grill over a medium-high charcoal fire or a gas grill set on high, or over high heat in a skillet. Poultry and pork burgers need to be cooked slightly longer, seafood burgers for a slightly shorter amount of time, both over medium-high heat.

THE MEAT

Chopped sirloin (around 10 percent fat) makes for really good burgers. Ground round (around 15 percent fat) makes for really *great* burgers. Ground chuck (20 percent fat) makes perhaps the best burgers. I used ground chuck on the outdoor grill with great success, but found it generated a bit too much fat in the pan when cooking burgers on the stove, so I went with ground round or sirloin when cooking in the skillet. Try to get your meat from a butcher shop where they grind the chopped meat fresh daily. It will cost a little more, but the freshness and integrity of the meat is worth it. If you can find organic or grass-fed beef, that's even better. Though they are on different ends of the culinary scale, think of the meat for your burgers as you would fish—buy the freshest possible, then cook it simply, in a way that encourages the essential flavor of the meat to flourish. Avoid frozen burger patties, which are about as satisfying as trying to have a serious conversation in a convertible.

DIMPLING

Burgers tend to shrink around the edges and puff in the middle as they cook. This has to do with a complicated litigation between the collagen and the muscle tissue, which is still being worked out in court. As the middle of the burger gets more rotund, it requires longer cooking time for the center to be medium-rare. By then the rest of the burger is well done. There is a simple solution: After shaping the burgers, make a ¼-inch dimple in the center of each burger with the tips of your middle three fingers. This will help maintain a uniform thickness during cooking and ensure a greater area of medium-rare burger, which is, after all, what we all want. Note that you can skip this process for the non-meat burgers, unless you find it enjoyable.

SALT

I find salting both sides of the burgers just before cooking preferable to adding the salt to the mixture before shaping, which requires excessive manipulation of the ingredients to incorporate the salt. (Some burgers are not salted because the ingredients added, such as sausage, already have sufficient seasoning.)

ACCOMPANIMENTS

Lettuce and tomato

Lettuce adds a cool, neutral complement to the meat. As for tomatoes, if it's a tasteless, Stepford tomato, why bother eating it? And if it's a really good tomato, why insist it compete with the brawny flavor of the burger? Tomato works with many of the lighter, non-beef burgers. Otherwise, it's better to cut the tomato in thick slices and serve these on the side sprinkled with sea salt.

Raw onion

Thinly sliced only! Avoid the inch-thick bar-burger onion slices, which only serve to devolve the burger itself into a condiment.

Toasted bun

For me, a toasted bun is like wearing a bow tie. I know there is a time and place for it, and that it suits some people well, but it's not for me.

Bun-to-meat ratio

The bun need not have a presence. Like Prufrock, it is "not Prince Hamlet, nor was it meant to be." The bun should be thought of simply as a burger delivery system. Too little bun is better than too much bun. I served most of the burgers here on packaged hamburger buns. I like them. They're soft. A crusty bun or bread will resist your bite, causing the burger to squash and release its juices, usually on your shirt. For some of the Adventurous Burgers, I had to think outside the bun and have included other bread choices, such as slices of country-style white bread, English muffins, pita, focaccia, and standard bakery rolls. You can supply your own thoughts. For instance, if you have a source for soft, slightly sweet Portuguese rolls, by all means employ them at will. I would.

Ketchup and/or mustard

Ketchup is the universal burger condiment. This has been proved recently by information returned to Earth from deep-space probes (Mars is red, after all). I've recommended alternatives to ketchup only when ketchup itself was inappropriate. Mayo and Thousand Island dressing should be used at your own discretion.

Condiments on top or bottom

Really up to the individual. Like pajamas, there's delight in wearing either.

Pickle

Always on the side. Put a pickle in with the burger, and its flavor will Proust you into a miasma of bad fast-food burger memories.

BURGER RULES

- Handle the meat as little as possible. Shape the burgers respectfully—don't pack them like snowballs. When mixing other ingredients into the meat, do it gently—as soon as they are incorporated, cease manipulating it.

- Do not pat or press burgers while they are cooking. You'll only succeed in pressing out the juices. Let cooking burgers lie.

- Turn the burgers only once. This also will help maintain their juiciness.

- When grilling burgers, always make sure you clean the grate beforehand.

Otherwise, the precious and flavorful burger crust you've worked so hard to achieve could stick to the grate during flipping.

• When cooking less fatty burgers, such as chicken or fish, on a barbecue grill, lightly oil the grate with a wad of paper towels dipped in vegetable oil just before cooking.

• Set up the plates with the buns or whatever bread you are using before you begin cooking. Also prep any condiments and either arrange them on the buns or have them handy. This way you can transfer the burgers directly from the grill onto the buns and serve them while they're still hot and at their most succulent.

BASIC COOKING INSTRUCTIONS

Stovetop Method

A well-seasoned cast-iron skillet is preferable. The burgers should not be touching in the pan, and always cook them uncovered. Covering the pan will steam the meat and make the crust soggy. Let the skillet get hot before cooking. This means placing it over high heat for about 2 minutes on a gas stove, slightly longer for electric, allowing for the coil to heat up. Add 1 tablespoon of vegetable oil and spread it evenly over the pan. Cook the burgers 5 minutes, flip, and cook 4 minutes more for medium-rare.

Charcoal Grill Method

Use enough coals to amply cover the bottom of the grill. Light them, preferably using the chimney method. Once the briquettes have ashed over, dump them over the bottom grate and arrange them in an even layer. Put the cooking grate in place and let it get hot for a minute, then brush it clean. Use a medium-high fire for the charcoal grill—the briquettes should be glowing through the ash and if you hold your hand about 3 inches over the grill, you should be able to stand the heat for only 4 seconds. Cook the burgers for 5 minutes, flip, and cook for 4 to 5 minutes more for medium-rare.

Gas Grill Method

Preheat with the cover down and all burners on high for about 15 minutes, or until the temperature reaches about 500°F (400°F for poultry and fish). Place the burgers on the grill and cook, covered, for 5 minutes. Turn and cook, covered, for 4 to 5 minutes more for medium-rare. (Gas grills usually need to be covered to retain the heat while cooking. Check the manufacturer's suggestions for your particular grill.) After cooking, turn off the heat, then immediately clean the grates with a wire brush while they are still hot.

CLASSIC BURGERS

HERE THEY ARE—THE STARTING LINEUP, THE ESSENTIAL BURGERS, the ones with the distinctive burger flavor that only comes from ground beef cooked over a hot fire until it is crusty on the outside and medium-rare and succulent on the inside. Amazingly, a perfectly cooked burger is hard to come by, which is why you are making them yourself. Though cooking a burger is always sublimely simple, you need to be completely focused. To this end, have the buns and ketchup ready, the drinks chilled, and the table set before you put the burgers on the heat. And have your favorite tunes playing, because when you're eating burgers, no melancholy is permitted.

The Burger

This is the iconic burger, the stuff that lunch and dinner dreams are made of. Like Ethel Merman singing, there's nothing held back, nothing enigmatic. Its flavor is out front, as intemperate as a sailor on a three-day pass.

1½ pounds ground round (see page 8)	1 tablespoon vegetable oil
Salt	4 hamburger buns

Gently shape the meat into 4 burgers about ¾ inch thick and 4 inches across. Make a ¼-inch dimple in the center of each burger with the tips of your middle three fingers. Sprinkle both sides with salt.

Place a skillet, preferably cast-iron, over high heat and let it get very hot, about 2 minutes. Add the oil and spread it evenly over the pan. Arrange the burgers so they aren't touching and cook, uncovered, for 5 minutes. Turn and cook about 4 minutes more for medium-rare, or as desired.

Remove the burgers from the pan, place on the buns, and serve.

For charcoal-grilled burgers, make a medium-hot fire (see page 12). Cook the burgers for 5 minutes. Turn and cook 4 to 5 minutes more.

For gas-grilled burgers, preheat on high until the grill is very hot, about 500°F. Cook the burgers for 5 minutes with the lid closed. Turn and cook 4 to 5 minutes more, again with the lid closed.

MAKES 4 BURGERS

The Cheeseburger

It's telling that *cheeseburger* is one word. It is not called a "burger with cheese," or "cheese atop a burger," but singularly and distinctly a *cheeseburger*. This suggests that in combination the two ingredients, meat and cheese, transcend the sum of their parts to such a degree that a new entity is born. It must be a burger with a *slice* of cheese melted on top. Cheese sauce poured over it or bits of cheese incorporated into the meat are not authentic. Choose a hard or semi-hard cheese that will complement the flavor of the meat and not be overwhelmed by it. Swiss, Cheddar, and Gruyère all melt well and have sufficient flavor.

1½ pounds ground round (see page 8)

Salt

1 tablespoon vegetable oil

4 thin slices Cheddar, Swiss, Gruyère, or other hard or semi-hard cheese

4 hamburger buns

Gently shape the meat into 4 burgers about ¾ inch thick and 4 inches across. Make a ¼-inch dimple in the center of each burger with the tips of your middle three fingers. Sprinkle both sides with salt.

Place a skillet, preferably cast-iron, over high heat and let it get very hot, about 2 minutes. Add the oil and spread it evenly over the pan. Arrange the burgers so they aren't touching and cook, uncovered, for 5 minutes. Turn and lay a slice of cheese over each burger. Do not cover. Cook about 4 minutes more for medium-rare, or as desired.

Serve on the hamburger buns.

For charcoal-grilled burgers, make a medium-hot fire (see page 12). Cook the burgers for 5 minutes. Turn, lay a slice of cheese on each burger, and cook 4 to 5 minutes more. The cheese may not melt entirely, but it will finish melting in the bun.

For gas-grilled burgers, preheat on high until the grill is very hot, about 500°F. Cook the burgers for 5 minutes with the lid closed. Turn, place a slice of cheese on each burger, and cook 4 to 5 minutes more, again with the lid closed.

MAKES 4 BURGERS

Portobello Mushroom and Goat Cheese Burger

I serve these on winter nights when I want a burger that has stateliness to it. The mushrooms in a balsamic reduction are the only condiment you'll need.

3 tablespoons olive oil

6 ounces portobello mushrooms (2 large mushrooms), stemmed and cut into ¼-inch slices

2 tablespoons balsamic vinegar

1 tablespoon fresh thyme leaves or 1 teaspoon dried

Salt

Freshly ground pepper

1½ pounds ground round (see page 8)

4 ounces goat cheese log, cut into four rounds about ¾-inch

4 hamburger buns or 8 slices of rustic white bread

Place a medium sauté pan over medium-high heat. Add 2 tablespoons of the olive oil and let it get hot, 1 to 2 minutes. Add the mushrooms and cook, stirring often, until softened, about 4 minutes. Stir in the balsamic vinegar well. Add the thyme and cook until the vinegar is almost gone, about 30 seconds. Season to taste with salt and pepper, remove from the heat, and set aside.

Gently shape the meat into 4 burgers about ¾ inch thick and 4 inches across. Make a ¼-inch dimple in the center of each burger with the tips of your middle three fingers. Sprinkle both sides with salt.

Place a skillet, preferably cast-iron, over high heat, add the remaining tablespoon of oil, and let it get very hot, about 2 minutes. Arrange the burgers so they aren't touching and cook, uncovered, for 5 minutes. Turn the burgers and place a round of goat cheese on the center of each burger. Cook, uncovered, 4 minutes more for medium-rare, or as desired.

Serve on the hamburger buns, topped with some of the portobello slices.

For charcoal-grilled burgers, make a medium-hot fire (see page 12). Cook the burgers for 5 minutes. Turn and lay a slice of cheese on top of each burger. Cook 4 to 5 minutes more.

For gas-grilled burgers, preheat on high until the grill is very hot, about 500°F. Cook the burgers for 5 minutes with the lid closed. Turn and lay a slice of cheese on top of each burger. Cook 4 to 5 minutes more, again with the lid closed.

MAKES 4 BURGERS

Blue Cheese Burger with Sautéed Onions

The *other* cheeseburger. Even those who do not care for blue cheese often find it irresistible in this combination. The sautéed onions add a touch of sweetness to complement the cheese.

3 tablespoons vegetable oil

2 medium onions, halved and cut lengthwise into thin slices

Salt

Freshly ground pepper

1½ pounds ground round (see page 8)

4 ounces blue cheese, crumbled into pea-sized pieces

4 hamburger buns

Ketchup

Thousand Island dressing

Place a large sauté pan over medium heat, add 2 tablespoons of the oil, and let it get hot, 1 to 2 minutes. Add the onion slices and cook, stirring often, until the onions soften, about 10 minutes. Season to taste with salt and pepper, remove from the heat, and set aside.

Place the ground beef in a medium bowl. Add the crumbled blue cheese and gently mix together until just combined. Shape the mixture into 4 burgers about ¾ inch thick and 4 inches across. Make a ¼-inch dimple in the center of each burger with the tips of your middle three fingers.

Place a skillet, preferably cast-iron, over high heat and let it get very hot, about 2 minutes. Add the remaining 1 tablespoon oil and spread it evenly over the pan. Arrange the burgers so they aren't touching and cook, uncovered, for 5 minutes. Turn and cook about 4 minutes more for medium-rare, or as desired.

Serve on the hamburger buns, topped with some of the sautéed onions and ketchup or Thousand Island dressing.

For charcoal-grilled burgers, make a medium-hot fire (see page 12). Cook the burgers for 5 minutes. Turn and cook 4 to 5 minutes more.

For gas-grilled burgers, preheat on high until the grill is very hot, about 500°F. Cook the burgers for 5 minutes with the lid closed. Turn and cook 3 to 4 minutes more, again with the lid closed.

MAKES 4 BURGERS

Meat Loaf Burger with Glazed Mushrooms

The best of both worlds, this burger has the flavor of meat loaf but is cooked like a burger. This means a considerably shorter cooking time, plus the benefit of the charred flavor picked up from the skillet or grill. Serve these burgers with Garlic Mashed Potatoes (page 83) and you'll have a more expeditious version of the classic Blue Plate Special. These are slightly more formidable than a basic burger, so you should serve them on a larger bakery roll or thick slices of challah or other hearty bread.

GLAZED MUSHROOMS

2 tablespoons olive oil

1 small onion, thinly sliced

12 ounces white or cremini mushrooms, stemmed and cut into 1/2-inch slices

2 tablespoons finely chopped garlic

1 tablespoon butter

2 tablespoons white wine

2 tablespoons chicken broth or water

1 tablespoon Worcestershire sauce

Freshly ground pepper

BURGERS

1/4 cup milk

1 slice white or whole-wheat bread, trimmed of crust and cut into 1-inch cubes

1 pound ground sirloin (see note)

1 small onion, finely chopped

1/4 cup freshly grated Parmesan cheese, preferably Parmigiano-Reggiano

1/4 cup chopped fresh parsley

1 large egg

2 tablespoons finely chopped garlic

2 tablespoons ketchup

1 tablespoon fresh thyme or 1 teaspoon dried

1 teaspoon Worcestershire sauce

Freshly ground pepper

1 tablespoon vegetable oil

4 bakery rolls or 8 thick slices of challah bread

To make the glazed mushrooms: Place a medium sauté pan over medium-high heat, add the olive oil, and let it get hot, about 1 minute. Add the onion and cook, stirring often, until it softens, about 4 minutes. Add the mushrooms and cook, stirring often, until the mushrooms soften, about 4 minutes more. Add the garlic and cook 1 minute more. Add the butter and stir until it is melted. Add the wine, chicken broth, Worcestershire sauce, and pepper to taste and stir until the mushrooms are glazed with the sauce. Remove from heat and set aside.

(continued)

To make the burgers: Put the milk in a small bowl. Add the bread cubes and mix together. Let the bread sit for a few minutes to soak up the milk.

Place the ground sirloin in a medium bowl. Add the soaked bread cubes and the rest of the burger ingredients and gently mix together until just combined. Shape the mixture into 4 burgers about ¾ inch thick and 4 inches across. Make a ¼-inch dimple in the center of each burger with the tips of your middle three fingers.

Place a skillet, preferably cast-iron, over high heat and let it get very hot, about 2 minutes. Add the oil and spread it evenly over the pan. Arrange the burgers so they aren't touching and cook, uncovered, for 5 minutes. Turn, reduce the heat to medium-high, and cook 4 to 5 minutes more for medium-rare, or as desired.

Serve on the rolls, topped with the mushroom-onion mixture.

For charcoal-grilled burgers, make a medium-hot fire (see page 12). Cook the burgers for 5 minutes. Turn and cook 4 to 5 minutes more.

For gas-grilled burgers, preheat on high until the grill is very hot, about 500°F. Cook the burgers for 5 minutes with the lid closed. Turn and cook 4 to 5 minutes more, again with the lid closed.

MAKES 4 BURGERS

Note: Use gound sirloin for this dish. Since the meat is being enhanced by the added flavors, it doesn't need as much fat content.

Bacon Cheeseburger

The bacon cheeseburger is a celebratory meal, reserved for special occasions—winning the big game, losing the big game, another day you're still alive and kicking. For neophyte chefs, especially the males of the species, it is often the first foray into cooking something complex, involving two steps—cooking the bacon, *then* making the burgers.

8 slices bacon

1½ pounds ground round (see page 8)

Salt

1 tablespoon vegetable oil

4 thin slices Cheddar, Swiss, Gruyère, or other hard or semi-hard cheese

4 hamburger buns

Place a skillet over medium-high heat and let it get hot, about 1 minute. Add the bacon slices and cook until lightly browned, about 3 minutes. Turn and cook to the desired crispness, 3 to 4 minutes more. Transfer the bacon to a plate lined with paper towels and pat gently to remove excess fat. Set aside.

Gently shape the meat into 4 burgers about ¾ inch thick and 4 inches across. Make a ¼-inch dimple in the center of each burger with the tips of your middle three fingers. Sprinkle both sides with salt.

Place a skillet, preferably cast-iron, over high heat and let it get very hot, about 2 minutes. Add the oil and spread it evenly over the pan. Arrange the burgers so they aren't touching and cook, uncovered, for 5 minutes. Turn and lay a slice of cheese over each burger. Do not cover. Cook about 4 minutes more for medium-rare, or as desired.

Remove the burgers from the pan, place on the buns, top each with 2 slices of bacon, and serve proudly.

For charcoal-grilled burgers, make a medium-hot fire (see page 12). Cook the burgers for 5 minutes. Turn, lay a slice of cheese on each burger, and cook 4 to 5 minutes more. The cheese may not melt entirely, but it will finish melting in the bun.

For gas-grilled burgers, preheat on high until the grill is very hot, about 500°F. Cook the burgers for 5 minutes with the lid closed. Turn, place a slice of cheese on each burger, and cook 4 to 5 minutes more, again with the lid closed.

MAKES 4 BURGERS

Pizza Burger

Do your best to find fresh mozzarella for this classic combo burger. The cheese will leak out while the burgers are cooking and turn crispy in the pan. Serve the tasty, golden brown bits with the burger.

3 tablespoons olive oil

8 ounces cremini or white mushrooms, stemmed and thinly sliced

4 ounces sweet Italian sausage, casing removed

½ cup prepared tomato sauce

1 tablespoon fresh oregano or 1 teaspoon dried

1½ pounds ground round (see page 8)

8 ounces fresh mozzarella, grated

Salt

Four 5-inch squares of focaccia or hamburger buns

¼ cup grated Parmesan cheese, preferably Parmigiano-Reggiano

Place a medium sauté pan over medium-high heat, add 2 tablespoons of the olive oil, and let it get hot, about 1 minute. Add the mushrooms and cook until they begin to soften, about 4 minutes. Add the sausage meat and cook until the meat is no longer pink, about 3 minutes, breaking the meat up into small pieces as it cooks. Add the tomato sauce and oregano and cook 1 minute more, stirring continuously. Remove the pan from the heat and set aside.

Place the ground beef in a medium bowl. Add the grated mozzarella and gently mix together until just combined. Shape the mixture into 4 burgers about ¾ inch thick and 4 inches across. Make a ¼-inch dimple in the center of each burger with the tips of your middle three fingers. Sprinkle both sides with salt.

Place a skillet over high heat and let it get very hot, about 2 minutes. Add the remaining 1 tablespoon olive oil and spread it evenly over the pan. Arrange the burgers so they aren't touching and cook, uncovered, for 5 minutes. Turn and cook about 4 minutes more for medium-rare, or as desired.

Serve on the squares of focaccia, cut in half widthwise, or on hamburger buns, topped with the mushroom-sausage mixture and a sprinkling of Parmesan.

For charcoal-grilled burgers, make a medium-hot fire (see page 12). Cook the burgers for 5 minutes. Turn and cook 4 to 5 minutes more.

For gas-grilled burgers, preheat on high until the grill is very hot, about 500°F. Cook the burgers for 5 minutes with the lid closed. Turn and cook 3 to 4 minutes more, again with the lid closed.

MAKES 4 BURGERS

ADVENTUROUS
BURGERS

I KNOW YOU'LL NEVER TIRE OF THE CLASSIC BURGER,
but, on occasion, you may grow restless and want some variation. These recipes push the burger envelope, giving you a wide range of flavors and international influences. They also utilize other meats besides beef, such as veal and pork. The ingredients may not, at first, seem like they jive with the idea of a burger, but they work beautifully. Preparations are somewhat more complex here, but the effort is always worth it. Most of these burgers are accompanied by their own distinctive sauce, as ketchup can be overwhelmed by some of the more exotic flavors.

Ancho Chile and Guacamole Burger

This is one majestic burger, with an explosion of earthy flavors. The smoky tones of the dried ancho chiles give this burger a dark, burly taste for which the ancho *mole* is the perfect condiment. Keep in mind the dried peppers take about 2 hours to reconstitute. If you like, you can serve these burgers on flour tortillas accompanied by rice and red beans and some margaritas.

8 strips bacon

GUACAMOLE

1 ripe avocado

2 tablespoons chopped red onion

2 tablespoons chopped fresh cilantro

2 tablespoons freshly squeezed lime juice, plus more if needed

1 tablespoon finely chopped garlic

Salt

BURGERS

3 dried ancho chiles

1 tablespoon vegetable oil

1 small red onion, finely chopped

3 tablespoons finely chopped garlic

4 scallions, green parts only, finely chopped

1 teaspoon salt

1½ pounds ground round (see page 8)

1 tablespoon vegetable oil

4 flour tortillas or hamburger buns

Place a skillet over medium-high heat and let it get hot, about 1 minute. Add the bacon slices and cook until lightly browned, about 3 minutes. Turn and cook to the desired crispness, 3 to 4 minutes more. Transfer the bacon to a plate lined with paper towels and pat gently to remove excess fat. Set aside.

To make the guacamole: Cut the avocado in half lengthwise, remove the pit, and scoop out the flesh into a medium bowl. Add the onion, cilantro, lime juice, garlic, and salt to taste. Mix together with a potato masher or the back of a fork until just combined. Do not overmix. Taste and add more lime juice, if desired. Lay plastic wrap directly over the surface of the guacamole, then cover the bowl and refrigerate until ready to use, or up to 4 hours.

To make the burgers: Soak the chiles in enough boiling water to cover for about 2 hours, or until they soften. You may need to weigh the chiles down with

(continued)

a small plate so they will be fully submerged. Once they are soft, stem, seed, and coarsely chop them. Place a medium sauté pan over medium-high heat, add the 1 tablespoon oil, and let it get hot, 1 to 2 minutes. Add the chopped chiles, onion, garlic, and scallions and cook, stirring frequently, until the onions soften, about 3 minutes. Stir in the 1 teaspoon salt.

Transfer $1/4$ cup of the chile mixture to the bowl of a blender or small food processor fitted with a steel blade. Transfer the remaining chile mixture to a medium bowl to cool. Add $1/4$ cup water to the blender and purée. Add more water, 1 teaspoon at a time, if necessary; the *mole* should be the consistency of ketchup. Transfer to a bowl and set aside, or cover and refrigerate for up to 1 day.

Add the ground beef to the bowl with the remaining cooled chile mixture and mix together until just combined. Gently shape the mixture into 4 burgers about $3/4$ inch thick and 4 inches across. Make a $1/4$-inch dimple in the center of each burger with the tips of your middle three fingers.

Place a skillet, preferably cast-iron, over high heat and let it get very hot, about 2 minutes. Add the 1 tablespoon oil and spread it evenly over the pan. Arrange the burgers so they aren't touching and cook, uncovered, for 5 minutes. Turn and cook about 4 minutes more for medium-rare, or as desired.

Serve each burger on a flour tortilla or bun topped with guacamole, 2 strips of bacon, and 2 tablespoons of *mole*.

For charcoal-grilled burgers, make a medium-hot fire (see page 12). Cook the burgers for 5 minutes. Turn and cook 4 to 5 minutes more.

For gas-grilled burgers, preheat on high until grill is very hot, about 500°F. Cook the burgers for 5 minutes with the lid closed. Turn and cook 4 to 5 minutes more, again with the lid closed.

MAKES 4 BURGERS

Lamb and Feta Burger
with Cumin-Yogurt Dressing

A grand marriage of Mediterranean flavors. The feta becomes more subdued as it cooks and provides a subtle infusion of tanginess. Make this burger with lamb or beef, depending on your mood. I've tried a variation of these burgers with the spinach mixed into the meat, but I prefer this preparation with the spinach cooked separately. These are especially good served in pita bread, drizzled with the Cumin-Yogurt Dressing. Mastering this burger is a real *feta accompli*.

SPINACH

2 tablespoons olive oil

12 ounces stemmed spinach leaves
  (preferably baby spinach)

1 tablespoon finely chopped garlic

1 teaspoon salt

Freshly ground pepper

CUMIN-YOGURT DRESSING

1 cup plain yogurt

1 tablespoon freshly squeezed
  lemon juice

1 teaspoon ground cumin

1 teaspoon curry powder

1 teaspoon ground ginger

1/2 teaspoon salt

BURGERS

1 pound ground lamb

4 ounces feta cheese, crumbled into
  pea-sized pieces

1/4 cup finely chopped onion

8 kalamata olives (scant 1/4 cup), pitted
  and finely chopped

3 tablespoons finely chopped garlic

2 tablespoons pine nuts

1 tablespoon chopped fresh oregano
  or 1 teaspoon dried

1 tablespoon vegetable oil

4 pita breads, at least 6 inches across

To make the spinach: Place a large sauté pan over medium-high heat, add the olive oil, and let it get hot, about 1 minute. Add the spinach and cook, stirring continuously, until it is wilted, about 3 minutes. (A pair of tongs works well for this.) Add the garlic, salt, and pepper to taste and cook 1 minute more, stirring continuously. Transfer to a platter and set aside.

To make the Cumin-Yogurt Dressing: Mix all the dressing ingredients together well in a small bowl. Taste and add more salt if needed. Keep refrigerated until ready to use.

(continued)

To make the burgers: Place the ground lamb in a medium bowl. Add the remaining burger ingredients and gently mix together until just combined. Shape the mixture into 4 burgers about ¾ inch thick and 4 inches across. Make a ¼-inch dimple in the center of each burger with the tips of your middle three fingers.

Place a skillet, preferably cast-iron, over high heat and let it get very hot, about 2 minutes. Add the oil and spread it evenly over the pan. Arrange the burgers so they aren't touching and cook, uncovered, for 5 minutes. Turn and cook about 4 minutes more for medium-rare, or as desired.

Serve in the pita bread, topped with the spinach mixture and drizzled with the Cumin-Yogurt Dressing.

For charcoal-grilled burgers, make a medium-hot fire (see page 12). Cook the burgers for 5 minutes. Turn and cook 4 to 5 minutes more.

For gas-grilled burgers, preheat on high until the grill is very hot, about 500°F. Cook the burgers for 5 minutes with the lid closed. Turn and cook 4 to 5 minutes more, again with the lid closed.

MAKES 4 BURGERS

Note: These burgers also can be made effectively with ground round instead of the ground lamb.

Bayou Burger

A provocative combination of spices and andouille sausage gives this burger a distinctive Cajun character.

BURGERS

1 pound ground lamb

1 andouille sausage (about 3 ounces), cut into ¼-inch pieces

½ cup finely chopped onion

3 tablespoons finely chopped garlic

1 large egg, lightly beaten

2 teaspoons Cajun or Creole seasoning (see note)

2 teaspoons mild chili powder

1 teaspoon ground cumin

½ teaspoon dried thyme

½ teaspoon dried basil

Freshly ground pepper

1 tablespoon vegetable oil

4 hamburger buns or soft French rolls

Lettuce

Red onion slices

Mayonnaise or Creole mustard

Place the ground lamb in a medium bowl. Add the remaining burger ingredients, including several grinds of pepper, and gently mix together until just combined. Shape the mixture into 4 burgers about ¾ inch thick and 4 inches across.

Place a skillet, preferably cast-iron, over high heat and let it get very hot, about 2 minutes. Add the oil and spread it evenly over the pan. Arrange the burgers so they aren't touching and cook, uncovered, for 5 minutes. Turn and cook about 4 minutes more for medium-rare, or as desired.

Remove the burgers from the pan and place on the buns. Serve with lettuce, a thin slice of red onion, and some mayo or Creole mustard.

For charcoal-grilled burgers, make a medium-hot fire (see page 12). Cook the burgers for 5 minutes. Turn and cook 4 to 5 minutes more.

For gas-grilled burgers, preheat on high until the grill is very hot, about 500°F. Cook the burgers for 5 minutes with the lid closed. Turn and cook 4 to 5 minutes more, again with the lid closed.

MAKES 4 BURGERS

Note: Creole or Cajun spice mixes are available in the spice section of most supermarkets. Try to find one with little or no salt added, as the sausage adds sufficient seasoning to the burger.

Tandoori Burger

This burger is cooked in a very hot oven, echoing the method of tandoori cooking. Its aroma, redolent of Indian spices, permeates the house whenever we make them. Serve it in Indian naan bread or pita bread.

1 pound ground lamb

¼ cup finely chopped onion

2 tablespoons finely chopped garlic

2 tablespoons finely chopped peeled fresh ginger

1 large egg

1 tablespoon curry powder

1 teaspoon salt

½ teaspoon ground coriander

½ teaspoon ground cumin

½ teaspoon cayenne pepper

4 pieces of naan bread or pita bread

Chopped lettuce

Tomato slices (or dices)

Onion slices

Cumin-Yogurt Dressing (page 31)

Preheat the oven to 500°F.

In a medium bowl, combine the lamb, onion, garlic, ginger, egg, curry powder, salt, coriander, cumin, and cayenne and gently mix together until just combined. Shape the mixture into 4 burgers about ¾ inch thick and 4 inches across.

Arrange the burgers in an ovenproof skillet so they aren't touching. Place the skillet on the center rack of the preheated oven and cook for 8 to 10 minutes, until the burgers are just a bit pink in the center, or about 160°F.

Serve in the naan bread (or pita bread as pictured opposite) with chopped lettuce, tomato, and onion and some Cumin-Yogurt Dressing.

MAKES 4 BURGERS

Thai Veal Burger

My kids love these burgers, finding them the perfect hybrid of Asian and backyard cuisines. They especially like the sweet-and-spicy glaze and demanded they be put in the book, even if these are not officially burgers, as they are served bun-less. These are half the size of a classic burger, so the cooking time is shorter.

SWEET-AND-SPICY SAUCE (see note)
¼ cup Japanese mirin wine

2 tablespoons water

1 tablespoon Thai red curry paste (see note)

1 tablespoon finely chopped garlic

1 tablespoon honey

2 teaspoons rice vinegar

Dash of hot sauce

BURGERS
1 tablespoon vegetable oil

¼ pound large shiitake mushrooms, stemmed and thinly sliced

Salt

Freshly ground pepper

1½ pounds ground veal

4 scallions, green parts only, finely chopped

¼ cup finely chopped peeled fresh ginger

¼ cup finely chopped garlic

3 tablespoons soy sauce

2 tablespoons Thai fish sauce (see note)

1 tablespoon Thai red curry paste

1 tablespoon vegetable oil

8 Boston or iceberg lettuce leaves

¼ cup sesame seeds for garnish

To make the Sweet-and-Spicy Sauce: Put all the sauce ingredients in a blender and purée until just smooth. Refrigerate until ready to use.

To make the burgers: Place a medium sauté pan over medium-high heat, add the 1 tablespoon oil, and let it get hot, about 1 minute. Add the mushroom slices and cook, stirring often, until they soften, about 5 minutes. Season to taste with salt and pepper. Transfer to a medium bowl and set aside to cool, about 10 minutes.

Add the veal to the bowl with the cooled mushrooms along with the scallions, ginger, garlic, soy sauce, fish sauce, and curry paste and gently mix together until just combined. Shape the mixture into 8 burgers about ½ inch thick and 3 inches across.

(continued)

Place a skillet, preferably cast-iron, over medium-high heat, add the 1 tablespoon of oil, and let it get hot, about 2 minutes. Arrange the burgers so they aren't touching and cook, uncovered, for 3 minutes. Turn and cook 3 minutes more. Add ¼ cup of the Sweet-and-Spicy Sauce to the pan. As it sizzles, use a pair of tongs to move and turn the burgers so both sides are nicely glazed.

Place 1 burger on each lettuce leaf and sprinkle with sesame seeds and a bit more of the sauce. Wrap the lettuce around the burgers, secure with toothpicks or hors d'oeuvres forks, and serve immediately.

MAKES 8 APPETIZER-SIZED BURGERS

Note: You can also use your favorite bottled Asian plum sauce or a Thai sweet chili sauce.

Note: Thai fish sauce and red curry paste are available in most specialty-food shops and in the Asian section of most supermarkets.

Surprise Burger

You might think the first bite of a perfectly cooked burger is surprise enough. But the Surprise Burger saves a little something extra for the middle—the unexpected treat of melted cheese and bacon, or one of the other variations. Kids like this idea, finding it a delightful marriage of surprise and burger. Make a moment out of it. Let them choose their own filling. Let them help make the burgers. Let them help set the table and do the dishes! Then they can go clean out the garage.

6 strips bacon	Salt
1½ pounds ground round (see page 8)	1 tablespoon vegetable oil
4 ounces Cheddar cheese, grated	4 hamburger buns

Place a skillet over medium-high heat and let it get hot, about 1 minute. Add the bacon slices and cook until lightly browned, about 4 minutes. Turn and cook to the desired crispness, 3 to 4 minutes more. Transfer the bacon to a plate lined with paper towels and pat gently to remove excess fat. When cool enough to handle, chop the bacon into ½-inch dice and set aside.

Divide the meat into 8 roughly equal portions. Press out each portion into a flat round about 4½ inches across. Pile about 1 tablespoon of chopped bacon in the center of 4 of the patties, being sure to keep about a ½ inch of space around the outside. Divide the grated cheese among the 4 patties, sprinkling it on top of the bacon.

Place a second patty of meat over each patty with bacon and cheese and press the edges together. Make a ¼-inch dimple in the center of each burger with the tips of your middle three fingers. Sprinkle both sides with salt.

Place a skillet, preferably cast-iron, over high heat and let it get very hot, about 2 minutes. Add the oil and spread it evenly over the pan. Arrange the burgers so they aren't touching and cook, uncovered, for 5 minutes. Turn and cook about 4 minutes more for medium-rare, or as desired.

Remove the burgers from the pan, place on the buns, and serve.

For charcoal-grilled burgers, make a medium-hot fire (see page 12). Cook the burgers for 5 minutes. Turn and cook 4 to 5 minutes more.

(continued)

For gas-grilled burgers, preheat on high until the grill is very hot, about 500°F. Cook the burgers for 5 minutes with the lid closed. Turn and cook 4 to 5 minutes more, again with the lid closed.

MAKES 4 BURGERS

Other Surprise Burger combos:
• Sautéed mushrooms and Gruyère cheese
• Chopped ham and Tallegio cheese
• Hot cappacola ham and provolone cheese
• Blue cheese and more blue cheese

Note: If you're making Surprise Burgers for the kids, accompany them with Egg Creams (page 91).

Negimaki Burger

I based this burger on the classic Japanese dish, where thinly sliced beef is rolled around scallions and finished with ginger sauce. This recipe puts all the ingredients together, which, after all, is what burgers are for.

GINGER SAUCE

¼ cup teriyaki sauce

¼ cup chicken broth or water

3 tablespoons finely chopped peeled fresh ginger

3 tablespoons finely chopped garlic

2 tablespoons freshly squeezed orange juice

1 tablespoon sesame oil

1 teaspoon curry powder

BURGERS

1½ pounds ground round (see page 8)

½ cup finely chopped scallions, green parts only

3 tablespoons finely chopped peeled fresh ginger

3 tablespoons finely chopped garlic

2 tablespoons teriyaki sauce

1 tablespoon vegetable oil

4 hamburger buns

To make the Ginger Sauce: In a small bowl, mix together all of the sauce ingredients and set aside.

To make the burgers: Place the ground round in a medium bowl. Add the remaining burger ingredients and gently mix together until just combined. Shape the mixture into 4 burgers about ¾ inch thick and 4 inches across. Make a ¼-inch dimple in the center of each burger with the tips of your middle three fingers.

Place a skillet, preferably cast-iron, over high heat and let it get very hot, about 2 minutes. Add the oil and spread it evenly over the pan. Arrange the burgers so they aren't touching and cook, uncovered, for 5 minutes. Turn and cook about 4 minutes more for medium-rare, or as desired.

Transfer the burgers to a platter.

Pour out any excess fat and then wipe the pan with paper towels. Add the Ginger Sauce and cook, stirring often, until it reduces by half and thickens, about 30 seconds. Pour the sauce over the burgers and serve on hamburger buns. Top with more Ginger Sauce, if desired.

(continued)

For charcoal-grilled burgers, make a medium-hot fire (see page 12). Cook the burgers for 5 minutes. Turn and cook 4 to 5 minutes more. Baste the top of each burger with Ginger Sauce, turn, and cook for 30 seconds. Baste again, turn, and cook for 30 seconds more (see note).

For gas-grilled burgers, preheat on high until the grill is very hot, about 500°F. Cook the burgers for 5 minutes with the lid closed. Turn and cook 4 to 5 minutes more, again with the lid closed. Baste the top of each burger with Ginger Sauce, turn, and cook for 30 seconds. Baste again, turn, and cook for 30 seconds more (see note).

MAKES 4 BURGERS

Note: In a small saucepan over medium heat, reduce the Ginger Sauce by half before using it to baste the charcoal- or gas-grilled burgers.

Picadillo Burger

If The Burger (page 15) is Sinatra, then this one is Louis Prima—same tunes, but done with more fire and abandon. The cinnamon and currants give the meat a brazen touch of sweetness. The chipotle sauce has a touch of heat. It may not become your favorite burger, but it could easily be your second.

CHIPOTLE SAUCE

1 tablespoon vegetable oil

1 medium onion, thinly sliced

3 tablespoons finely chopped garlic

1 poblano chile, stemmed, seeded, and coarsely chopped

1 chipotle chile in adobo sauce, coarsely chopped (see note)

1 tablespoon chili powder

1 cup chicken broth

½ teaspoon salt

BURGERS

1½ pounds ground round (see page 8)

½ cup finely chopped onion

6 green olives, pitted and finely chopped

3 tablespoons currants soaked for 10 minutes in hot water, then drained and coarsely chopped

3 tablespoons finely chopped garlic

1 tablespoon chili powder

1 teaspoon ground cumin

1 teaspoon ground coriander

1 teaspoon salt, plus more for sprinkling

½ teaspoon cinnamon

½ teaspoon nutmeg

1 tablespoon vegetable oil

4 hamburger buns

To make the Chipotle Sauce: Place a medium sauté pan over medium heat, add the 1 tablespoon oil, onion, garlic, and poblano chile and cook slowly until the vegetables soften, about 8 minutes. Add the chipotle chile and chili powder and cook 30 seconds more, stirring steadily. Add the chicken broth and salt and bring to a simmer. Reduce the heat to medium-low and simmer until the liquid reduces by half, 2 to 3 minutes. Transfer the sauce to the bowl of a blender or small food processor fitted with a steel blade and purée. Set aside or refrigerate for up to 1 day.

To make the burgers: Place the ground round in a medium bowl. Add the remaining burger ingredients and gently mix together until just combined. Shape the mixture into 4 burgers about ¾ inch thick and 4 inches across. Make

(continued)

a ¼-inch dimple in the center of each burger with the tips of your middle three fingers. Sprinkle both sides with salt.

Place a skillet, preferably cast-iron, over high heat and let it get very hot, about 2 minutes. Add the 1 tablespoon oil and spread it evenly over the pan. Arrange the burgers so they aren't touching and cook, uncovered, for 5 minutes. Turn and cook about 4 minutes more for medium-rare, or as desired.

Serve on the hamburger buns, topped with a generous portion of the Chipotle Sauce.

For charcoal-grilled burgers, make a medium-hot fire (see page 12). Cook the burgers for 5 minutes. Turn and cook 4 to 5 minutes more.

For gas-grilled burgers, preheat on high until the grill is very hot, about 500°F. Cook the burgers for 5 minutes with the lid closed. Turn and cook 4 to 5 minutes more, again with the lid closed.

MAKES 4 BURGERS

Note: Chipotle chiles packed in adobo sauce are available in Hispanic markets and most specialty-food shops. Do not rinse before using; any clinging sauce is welcome.

Morel Burger

Perhaps you're thinking, why waste some precious morels on a burger? Or maybe you're thinking, why overwhelm a decent burger with morels? But try this burger once and you'll understand. Assemble the patties in the morning and let them sit covered in the fridge for the day. This will help the veal to be infused with the piquant flavor of the morels. Though still a burger, when topped with the luxurious cream sauce, it's transformed into something splendid, like when one of the racetrack regulars finally picks a long shot that actually wins. Serve on rounds cut from the center of a slice of decent toasted white bread. Pair these with the Rosemary Roasted Potatoes (page 80).

1 ounce dried morels (see note)

2 tablespoons olive oil

1 tablespoon butter

1 teaspoon salt, plus more for seasoning

Freshly ground pepper

1 pound ground veal

$\frac{1}{4}$ cup finely chopped shallots

$\frac{1}{4}$ cup dry white wine

$\frac{1}{2}$ cup heavy cream

2 tablespoons finely chopped fresh parsley

8 slices white bread, toasted and trimmed into 4-inch rounds

Chopped chives for garnish

Soak the morels in warm water in a small bowl for 1 hour. Strain them, saving the liquid. Rinse the morels gently, looking to remove any pieces of dirt in the folds. Transfer to paper towels and gently pat dry.

Place a medium sauté pan over medium-high heat. Add 1 tablespoon of the olive oil and the butter. Just when the butter stops sizzling, add the morels and cook until they begin to get a bit crispy around the edges, about 5 minutes. Season with salt and pepper.

Reserve half of the morels. Chop the remaining ones coarsely and transfer to a medium bowl.

Add the veal to the bowl with the chopped morels. Sprinkle on the 1 teaspoon salt and gently mix together until just combined. Shape the mixture into 4 burgers about $\frac{3}{4}$ inch thick and 4 inches across. Make a $\frac{1}{4}$-inch dimple in the center of each burger with the tips of your middle three fingers.

Place a skillet, preferably cast-iron, over high heat and let it get very hot, about 2 minutes. Add the remaining 1 tablespoon olive oil and spread it evenly over the pan. Arrange the burgers so they aren't touching and cook, uncovered,

(continued)

for 5 minutes. Turn and cook about 4 minutes more. They should be just a bit pink in the center, or about 160°F. Transfer the burgers to a plate.

Add the shallots and reserved morels to the pan and cook, stirring continuously, until the shallots soften, about 1 minute. Add the wine and stir until it is reduced by half, about 1 more minute. Add the cream and cook, stirring continuously, until the sauce reduces by half and starts to thicken, about 2 minutes. Stir in the parsley. Season with salt and pepper.

For presentation, set a toast round just off the center of each plate. Arrange a burger half-off each toast round. Top with the cream sauce, making sure the morels are evenly distributed among each plate. Top with the remaining toast circles, leaning them against the burgers at a rakish angle. Garnish with chopped chives and serve immediately. This is the one burger in this book you probably want to eat with a knife and fork.

MAKES 4 BURGERS

Note: Fresh morels are available in the spring and can be substituted for dried. Use $\frac{1}{4}$ pound fresh morels for 1 ounce dried. Morels are a bit expensive, but fresh or dried, their flavor is unique and is close to the intensity of a truffle.

Churasco Burger with Chimichurri Sauce

You can put this classic Argentine green sauce on just about any steak or roasted chicken and it suddenly hulks and becomes a dish to be reckoned with. This burger evokes Argentine barbecue (*churasco*), but with a lot less hassle.

CHIMICHURRI SAUCE
1 cup packed fresh Italian parsley
  leaves

1 cup packed fresh mint leaves

⅓ cup olive oil

¼ cup freshly squeezed lemon juice

3 tablespoons finely chopped garlic

1 tablespoon red pepper flakes

1 teaspoon ground cumin

1 teaspoon salt

BURGERS
1½ pounds ground round (see page 8)

½ cup finely chopped onion

¼ cup finely chopped fresh parsley

¼ cup finely chopped fresh mint

3 tablespoons finely chopped garlic

1 tablespoon red pepper flakes

1 teaspoon ground cumin

1 teaspoon dried oregano

Salt

1 tablespoon vegetable oil

4 pita breads

Red onion slices

To make the Chimichurri Sauce: Place all the sauce ingredients in the bowl of a food processor fitted with a steel blade and process until smooth. Set aside until ready to use. The sauce can be kept for up to 2 days in the refrigerator in a well-sealed container.

To make the burgers: Place the ground round in a medium bowl. Add all of the remaining burger ingredients except the salt and gently mix together until just combined. Shape the mixture into 4 burgers about ¾ inch thick and 4 inches across. Make a ¼-inch dimple in the center of each burger with the tips of your middle three fingers. Sprinkle both sides with salt.

Place a skillet, preferably cast-iron, over high heat and let it get very hot, about 2 minutes. Add the oil and spread it evenly over the pan. Arrange the burgers so they aren't touching and cook, uncovered, for 5 minutes. Turn and cook 4 to 5 minutes more for medium-rare, or as desired.

Serve in the pita breads, topped with thinly sliced red onion and some Chimichurri Sauce.

For charcoal-grilled burgers, make a medium-hot fire (see page 12). Cook the burgers for 5 minutes. Turn and cook 4 to 5 minutes more.

For gas-grilled burgers, preheat on high until the grill is very hot, about 500°F. Cook the burgers for 5 minutes with the lid closed. Turn and cook 4 to 5 minutes more, again with the lid closed.

MAKES 4 BURGERS

Barbecued Pork Burger

This burger captures the spirit of an authentic down-home pulled-pork barbecue sandwich. Let the sauce soak into the bun and eat it with a fork. It will definitely give you a heady barbecue rush. Top with Classic Cole Slaw (page 87) for a real southern treat.

1½ pounds ground pork

¼ cup finely chopped onion

3 tablespoons finely chopped garlic

2 tablespoons prepared barbecue sauce, plus extra for garnish

1 tablespoon Dijon mustard

1 tablespoon sweet paprika

1 tablespoon chili powder

½ teaspoon liquid smoke (optional)

1 tablespoon vegetable oil

4 hamburger buns

Place the ground pork in a medium bowl. Add all the onion, garlic, 2 tablespoons barbecue sauce, the mustard, paprika, chili powder, and liquid smoke (if using) and gently mix together until just combined. Shape the mixture into 4 burgers about ¾ inch thick and 4 inches across. Make a ¼-inch dimple in the center of each burger with the tips of your middle three fingers.

Place a skillet, preferably cast-iron, over high heat and let it get very hot, about 2 minutes. Add the oil and spread it evenly over the pan. Arrange the burgers so they aren't touching and cook, uncovered, for 5 minutes. Turn and cook 4 to 5 minutes more, or until the meat is no longer pink inside, or about 160°F.

Serve in the hamburger buns, topped with additional barbecue sauce.

For charcoal-grilled burgers, make a medium-hot fire (see page 12). Cook the burgers for 5 minutes. Turn and cook 4 to 5 minutes more.

For gas-grilled burgers, preheat on high until the grill is very hot, about 500°F. Cook the burgers for 5 minutes with the lid closed. Turn and cook 4 to 5 minutes more, again with the lid closed.

MAKES 4 BURGERS

Merguez Burger

Maybe you have a friend who, as soon as they arrive at a party, immediately lights up the room and turns the event into something special. *Merguez,* spicy Morrocan-style lamb sausage alive with Middle Eastern spices, is like that. Whatever dish you use it in is transformed with exotic flavor. It feels a little like cheating, it's so good. You can find *merguez* sausage in some specialty-food shops, or you can search for it on the Internet.

12 ounces ground lamb

12 ounces *merguez* sausage, casing removed

¼ cup finely chopped onion

2 tablespoons finely chopped garlic

1 tablespoon vegetable oil

4 pita breads at least 6 inches across

Cumin-Yogurt Dressing (page 31)

Place the ground lamb in a medium bowl. Add the sausage, onion, and garlic and mix together, breaking up the sausage meat so it is evenly incorporated into the ground lamb. Shape the mixture into 4 burgers about ¾ inch thick and 4 inches across.

Place a skillet, preferably cast-iron, over high heat and let it get very hot, about 2 minutes. Add the oil and spread it evenly over the pan. Arrange the burgers so they aren't touching and cook, uncovered, for 5 minutes. Turn and cook about 4 minutes more for medium-rare, or as desired.

Serve in pita bread, drizzled with Cumin-Yogurt Dressing.

For charcoal-grilled burgers, make a medium-hot fire (see page 12). Cook the burgers for 5 minutes. Turn and cook 4 to 5 minutes more.

For gas-grilled burgers, preheat on high until the grill is very hot, about 500°F. Cook the burgers for 5 minutes with the lid closed. Turn and cook 4 to 5 minutes more, again with the lid closed.

MAKES 4 BURGERS

Note: No need to salt these, as the sausage already adds sufficient seasoning to the burger.

A-LITTLE-LIGHTER
BURGERS

THESE BURGERS ARE USUALLY LIGHTER AND HAVE LESS FAT

than the Classic or Adventurous Burgers. They are also more delicate, and you should not speak to them harshly or flip them in the pan too brusquely, as they might not hold together. These are probably not the burgers you would grill while tailgating before the big game. And, though it's not in keeping with the usual burger zeitgeist, you might feel like serving a decent wine with them, which is fine. The fish or seafood burgers require a slightly lower flame—usually medium-high—so as not to overcook the outside before the inside is done. Because the burgers are more delicate, if you want to cook them on the barbecue, make sure the grate is very clean and lightly oiled. Refrigerating the burgers for at least an hour will also help hold them together. An even better method is to cook them in one of the grill pans designed for grilling vegetables. These rest right on the grates and will give you a flat surface better suited for grilling these burgers.

Pollo Reggiano Burger

My wife and I spent our honeymoon in Reggio Emilia in Northern Italy. It wound up lasting six months. We didn't eat any burgers there. We did have *molto* prosciutto, Gorgonzola, Parmigiano-Reggiano, and basil in various combinations. Since Reggio is home to no imposing *duomo,* no major museum or Roman ruins, the main thing to do is eat—which we did, often and well. I devised this burger in homage to that wonderful time.

PESTO

3 cups packed fresh basil leaves, well dried

¼ cup extra-virgin olive oil

¼ cup freshly grated Parmesan cheese, preferably Parmigiano-Reggiano

BURGERS

1½ pounds skinless boneless chicken thighs (about 3 pounds bone-in), cut into 1-inch pieces

2 ounces prosciutto, chopped into medium dice

2 ounces sweet Gorgonzola cheese, crumbled

¼ cup finely chopped roasted red bell pepper (see note)

¼ cup plain dried bread crumbs

¼ cup freshly grated Parmesan cheese, preferably Parmigiano Reggiano

2 tablespoons chopped fresh basil or 2 teaspoons dried

1 tablespoon prepared sundried tomato pesto

1 teaspoon salt

2 tablespoons olive oil

4 five-inch squares focaccia, cut in half widthwise

To make the pesto: Put the basil and extra-virgin olive oil in a blender or food processor fitted with a steel blade and pulse until the basil is a smooth purée. Add the Parmesan and pulse to combine. Transfer to a bowl and set aside.

To make the burgers: Combine all of the burger ingredients in the bowl of a food processor fitted with a steel blade and pulse until the chicken is the consistency of ground beef, about 8 pulses. Gently shape the mixture into 4 burgers about ¾ inch thick and 4 inches across. The mixture will be a little loose. Wash hands well.

Place a skillet, preferably cast-iron, over medium-high heat, add the olive oil, and let it get hot, about 2 minutes. Arrange the burgers so they aren't touching

(continued)

and cook, uncovered, for 6 minutes. Turn and cook 5 to 6 minutes more, until no longer pink in the center, or about 165°F.

Transfer the burgers to the focaccia pieces and top with the pesto.

If cooking these on a grill, refrigerate the burgers for at least an hour and make sure the grate is clean and well oiled. Also brush the burgers lightly with oil before placing them on the grate.

For charcoal-grilled burgers, make a medium-hot fire (see page 12). Cook the burgers for 6 minutes. Turn and cook 5 to 6 minutes more.

For gas-grilled burgers, preheat on high until the grill is medium hot, about 400°F. Cook the burgers for 6 minutes with the lid closed. Turn and cook 5 to 6 minutes more, again with the lid closed.

MAKES 4 BURGERS

Note: To roast bell peppers, place them directly over the flame on a gas stove or grill, turning as the bottom gets blackened. When the entire pepper is charred, place in a heavy brown paper bag or in a covered bowl and let it sit for 20 minutes. The charred skin can then be easily peeled away and the stem, seeds, and ribs removed. You may substitute good-quality jarred roasted red peppers; drain thoroughly before using.

Salmon Burger with Spicy Ginger Sauce

This may well become your favorite way to cook salmon. You'll never have to suffer through another dry, bland salmon steak again with these moist and flavorful burgers. They can be assembled in the morning—just wrap each one individually in plastic and refrigerate.

SPICY GINGER SAUCE
¼ cup chicken stock

¼ cup Chinese plum sauce

2 tablespoons finely chopped peeled fresh ginger

2 tablespoons finely chopped garlic

1 teaspoon cornstarch dissolved in 1 tablespoon water

½ teaspoon spicy Asian chili sauce or other hot sauce

BURGERS
1½ pounds salmon fillets, skinned, boned, and cut into 3-inch cubes

½ cup finely chopped onion

¼ cup chopped fresh cilantro

3 scallions, green parts only, coarsely chopped

2 tablespoons finely chopped garlic

2 tablespoons finely chopped peeled fresh ginger

2 tablespoons sesame oil

2 tablespoons Thai fish sauce (see note)

1 tablespoon soy sauce

1 tablespoon curry powder

1 teaspoon finely chopped jalapeño pepper

2 tablespoons vegetable oil

4 brioche rolls or hamburger buns

To make the Spicy Ginger Sauce: In a small bowl, mix together all of the sauce ingredients and set aside.

To make the burgers: Combine all of the burger ingredients in the bowl of a food processor fitted with a steel blade and pulse until the salmon is the consistency of ground beef, about 6 pulses. Do not overprocess.

Gently shape the mixture into 4 burgers about ¾ inch thick and 4 inches across. Set these on a plate so they are not touching, cover well with plastic wrap, and refrigerate for at least 1 hour.

Place a skillet, preferably cast-iron, over medium-high heat and let it get hot, about 2 minutes. Add the vegetable oil and spread it evenly over the pan. Arrange the burgers so they aren't touching and cook, uncovered, for 5 minutes. Turn and cook 4 to 5 minutes more, until just cooked through.

(continued)

Transfer the burgers to a platter and scrape any bits of burger from the pan. Return the pan to medium-high heat, add the Spicy Ginger Sauce, and cook for two minutes until the sauce thickens slightly.

Serve the burgers on the brioche rolls, topped with the Spicy Ginger Sauce.

For charcoal-grilled burgers, make a medium-hot fire (see page 12). Cook the burgers for 5 minutes. Turn and cook 4 to 5 minutes more.

For gas-grilled burgers, preheat on high until the grill is very hot, about 400°F. Cook the burgers for 5 minutes with the lid closed. Turn and cook 4 to 5 minutes more, again with the lid closed.

MAKES 4 BURGERS

Note: Fish sauce is one of the staples of Thai cuisine and imparts its distinctive flavor to many dishes. It should be available in specialty-food shops and in the Asian section of many supermarkets. Keep it in the refrigerator after opening.

Note: In a small saucepan, cook the Spicy Ginger Sauce for two minutes over medium-high heat before serving with the charcoal- or gas-grilled burgers.

Island Shrimp Burger

This burger is flush with citrus and island spices. It requires a bit of work to assemble and a gentle hand when turning, but the result is something memorable.

2 tablespoons vegetable oil

2 tablespoons butter

½ cup finely chopped onion

¼ cup finely chopped red bell pepper

1 pound large shrimp, shelled, deveined, and chopped in ¼-inch pieces

¼ cup chopped fresh cilantro

3 scallions, green parts only, finely chopped

2 tablespoons finely chopped garlic

2 tablespoons finely chopped peeled fresh ginger

1 tablespoon fresh thyme or 1 teaspoon dried

1½ teaspoons cayenne pepper

1 teaspoon ground allspice

½ teaspoon grated lime zest

2 tablespoons freshly squeezed lime juice

2 tablespoons freshly squeezed orange juice

1 teaspoon salt

1 cup dried bread crumbs

3 eggs

1 cup all-purpose flour

4 hamburger buns

Mayonnaise

Hot sauce

Place a large skillet over medium heat and add 1 tablespoon of the oil and 1 tablespoon of the butter. When the butter is melted, add the onion and bell pepper and cook, stirring often, until they soften, about 6 minutes. Raise the heat to high and add the chopped shrimp, cilantro, scallions, garlic, ginger, thyme, cayenne, allspice, and lime zest. Cook, stirring often, until the shrimp is almost cooked through, about 2 minutes. Add the lime juice, orange juice, and salt and cook 1 minute longer.

Transfer the shrimp mixture with a slotted spoon to a medium bowl. Reduce any liquid left in the pan until it thickens, then transfer to the bowl with the shrimp. Let the mixture cool.

Add ½ cup of the bread crumbs and 1 of the eggs to the shrimp mixture and mix together until well combined. Shape the mixture into 4 burgers about ¾ inch thick and 4 inches across. The mixture will be loose. Arrange the burgers on a platter so they aren't touching, cover gently with plastic, and refrigerate for at least 1 hour or up to 6 hours.

Put the flour in a large, shallow bowl or pie plate. Beat the remaining 2 eggs in a bowl. Put the remaining $\frac{1}{2}$ cup bread crumbs in a large, shallow bowl or pie plate. Dredge the chilled shrimp burgers in the flour so they are lightly dusted on both sides. Dip them into the eggs, then dredge them in the bread crumbs so they are lightly coated.

Place a skillet, preferably cast-iron, over medium-high heat and add the remaining 1 tablespoon each oil and butter. Just when the butter stops sizzling, arrange the shrimp burgers in the pan so they aren't touching and cook, uncovered, for 3 minutes, until a nice crust forms on the bottom. Turn carefully and cook about 3 minutes more.

Serve on the hamburger buns, topped with some mayo and your choice of hot sauce.

MAKES 4 BURGERS

Note: These burgers are too delicate to cook on an outdoor grill.

Jerk Chicken Burger

I once had some jerk chicken at a roadside stand in Montego Bay, Jamaica, that was such a salacious display of flavor, I am somewhat hesitant to invoke the "jerk" moniker here. But this burger, while not the same kind of licentious eruption of taste, is far from chaste. It sports a lively tang and just enough heat to merit the chilling of several beers.

JERK SAUCE

3 scallions, green parts only, roughly cut into 3-inch lengths

¼ cup hot sauce made from Scotch bonnet peppers (see note)

¼ cup packed fresh parsley leaves

¼ cup freshly squeezed orange juice

¼ cup freshly squeezed lime juice

2 tablespoons Dijon mustard

½ tablespoon white vinegar

½ teaspoon ground allspice

½ teaspoon cinnamon

BURGERS

1½ pounds skinless boneless chicken thighs (about 3 pounds bone-in), cut into 1-inch pieces

3 cloves garlic

1 teaspoon salt

2 tablespoons vegetable oil

4 hamburger buns

Lettuce leaves

Red onion slices

To make the jerk sauce: Put all the sauce ingredients in a food processor fitted with a steel blade and purée. Transfer to a medium bowl and set aside for 2 hours to allow the flavors to intensify, or refrigerate overnight.

To make the burgers: In the bowl of a food processor fitted with a steel blade, combine the chicken, garlic, and salt. Add 6 tablespoons of the jerk sauce and pulse until the chicken is the consistency of ground beef, about 8 pulses. Gently shape the mixture into 4 burgers about ¾ inch thick and 4 inches across. The mixture will be loose.

Place a skillet, preferably cast-iron, over medium-high heat and let it get hot, about 2 minutes. Add the oil and spread it evenly over the pan. Arrange the burgers so they aren't touching and cook, uncovered, for 6 minutes. Turn and cook 5 to 6 minutes more, until no longer pink in the center, or about 165°F.

Serve on the hamburger buns, topped with the lettuce, red onion slices, and additional jerk sauce.

For charcoal-grilled burgers, make a medium-hot fire (see page 12). Cook the burgers for 5 minutes. Turn and cook about 5 minutes more.

For gas-grilled burgers, preheat on high until the grill is very hot, about 500°F. Cook the burgers for 5 minutes with the lid closed. Turn and cook about 5 minutes more, again with the lid closed.

MAKES 4 BURGERS

Note: Hot sauce made from Scotch bonnet peppers, also known as habañeros, is available in most specialty-food shops.

Chicken and Plantain Burger
with Pecan Crust

One of my favorite things to eat is called a *pianono,* which is a complicated Jamaican dish made by forming a ring from a slice of sautéed plantain and filling it with a spicy ground chicken mixture, then frying the whole thing. This version is far simpler and combines all those wonderful flavors. To help keep the pecans from scorching, once the burger is flipped, cover the pan and reduce the flame to low.

1 ripe plantain (see note)

1 tablespoon butter

1 pound skinless boneless chicken thighs (about 2 pounds bone-in), cut into 1-inch pieces (see note)

2 ounces smoked ham or Canadian bacon, cut into small dice

2 scallions, green parts only, coarsely chopped

6 green olives, pitted and coarsely chopped

¼ cup coarsely chopped fresh parsley

2 tablespoons plain dried bread crumbs

1 large egg

1 teaspoon salt

½ teaspoon ground cumin

½ teaspoon ground allspice

½ teaspoon dried oregano

Freshly ground pepper to taste

6 ounces (about 2 cups) pecan halves

2 tablespoons vegetable oil

4 Portuguese rolls or hamburger buns

Mango Ketchup (page 72)

Peel the plantain and cut it lengthwise into ½-inch slices.

Place a large sauté pan over medium-high heat and add the butter. When the butter stops sizzling, arrange the plantain slices in a single layer and cook until they are lightly browned on the bottom, about 1 minute. Turn and cook 1 minute more. Transfer to a plate and let them cool, then coarsely chop them.

In the bowl of a food processor fitted with a steel blade, combine the chopped plantains with the chicken pieces, ham, scallions, olives, parsley, bread crumbs, egg, salt, cumin, allspice, oregano, and pepper to taste. Pulse until all the ingredients are just chopped and the chicken is the consistency of ground beef, about 8 pulses. Shape the mixture into 4 burgers about ¾ inch thick and 4 inches across. Arrange on a platter, cover with plastic, and refrigerate for at least 1 hour or up to 6 hours.

While the burgers are chilling, place the pecans in the bowl of a food processor fitted with a steel blade and pulse until the pecans are finely chopped, about the size of split peas. Do not overprocess. (The pecans can also be chopped with a knife.) Transfer to a pie plate. Dredge each chilled burger in the pecans so they are lightly coated with the nuts on each side.

Place a skillet, preferably cast-iron, over medium heat, add the oil, and let it get hot, about 2 minutes. Arrange the burgers so they aren't touching and cook, uncovered, for 6 minutes. Turn the burgers carefully, reduce the heat to medium-low, cover the pan, and cook 5 to 6 minutes more, until no longer pink in the center, or about 165°F.

Serve on the sweet Portuguese rolls, topped with Mango Ketchup.

MAKES 4 BURGERS

Note: These burgers are too delicate to cook on an outdoor grill.

Note: Ripe plantains are a deep yellow color with some areas of dark brown or black (as opposed to unripe plantains, which are green). Don't worry about the dark areas; as long as the plantain is not mushy, it is fine to use.

Note: You can make this recipe substituting 1 pound of store-bought ground chicken for the chicken thighs. Place the ground chicken in a medium bowl. Combine the remaining burger ingredients in the food processor and chop finely. Add that mixture to the ground chicken and mix together until just combined. Shape into burgers and continue with the recipe.

Breakfast Burger

Not your father's breakfast. Shape these into burgers the night before, then throw them in a pan the next morning for a quick, nutritious, filling, and novel way to start the day. Scramble an egg while the burgers are frying and add it to the sandwich.

1 pound skinless boneless chicken thighs (about 2 pounds bone-in), cut into 1-inch pieces (see note, page 67)

¼ cup diced smoked Canadian bacon (about 4 ounces)

1 tart apple such as Granny Smith, peeled, cored, and cut into large dice

¼ cup coarsely chopped onion

2 tablespoons maple syrup

2 teaspoons dried sage

1 teaspoon salt

½ teaspoon red pepper flakes

¼ teaspoon ground cloves

¼ teaspoon ground allspice

2 tablespoons vegetable oil

4 slices Cheddar cheese

4 English muffins, toasted

4 large eggs, scrambled

In the bowl of a food processor fitted with a steel blade, combine the chicken pieces with the Canadian bacon, apple, onion, maple syrup, sage, salt, red pepper flakes, cloves, and allspice. Pulse until all the ingredients are just chopped and the chicken is the consistency of ground beef, about 8 pulses. Shape the mixture into 4 burgers about ½ inch thick and 4 inches across (these will be a bit thinner than a regular burger). The mixture will be a little loose.

Place the burgers on a platter, cover with plastic, and refrigerate until ready to use.

Place a skillet, preferably cast-iron, over medium-high heat and let it get hot, about 2 minutes. Add the oil and spread it evenly over the pan. Arrange the burgers so they aren't touching and cook, uncovered, for 6 minutes. Turn and lay a slice of cheese over each burger. Do not cover. Cook 5 to 6 minutes more, until no longer pink in the center, or about 165°F.

Serve on the toasted English muffins, topping each with a scrambled egg.

MAKES 4 BURGERS

Southwestern Turkey Burger

Turkey burgers have the reputation of being, well, turkey burgers—dry and dull and characterized only by a paucity of flavor. These turkey burgers defy the norm. They are juicy and flavorful, and the sausage gives them an extra bounce. Turn them carefully in the pan to help maintain the integrity of their burgerness.

1 pound ground turkey

1 Southwestern or Cajun-style smoked chicken sausage (about 4 ounces), cut into ¼-inch pieces

1 cup canned corn kernels, well drained

¼ cup finely chopped onion

¼ cup finely chopped roasted red bell pepper (see note, page 58)

3 tablespoons prepared salsa, plus more for garnish

3 tablespoons finely chopped garlic

2 tablespoons chili powder

½ teaspoon finely chopped jalapeño pepper (optional)

Freshly ground pepper

2 tablespoons vegetable oil

8 slices white bread or 4 hamburger buns

Lettuce leaves (optional)

Red onion slices (optional)

In a medium bowl, combine the ground turkey, sausage, corn, onion, roasted bell pepper, 3 tablespoons salsa, garlic, chili powder, jalapeño (if using), and several grinds of pepper. Gently mix together until just combined. Shape the mixture into 4 burgers about ¾ inch thick and 4 inches across.

Place a skillet, preferably cast-iron, over medium-high heat, add the oil, and let it get hot, about 2 minutes. Arrange the burgers so they aren't touching and cook, uncovered, for 6 minutes. Turn and cook 5 to 6 minutes more, until no longer pink in the center, or about 165°F.

Transfer to the bread slices. Top with salsa, lettuce, and red onion and serve.

If cooking these on a grill, refrigerate the burgers for at least an hour and make sure the grate is clean and well oiled. Also brush the burgers lightly with oil before placing them on the grate.

For charcoal-grilled burgers, make a medium-hot fire (see page 12). Cook the burgers for 6 minutes. Turn and cook about 5 minutes more.

For gas-grilled burgers, preheat on high until the grill is hot, about 400°F. Cook the burgers for 6 minutes with the lid closed. Turn and cook about 5 minutes more, again with the lid closed.

MAKES 4 BURGERS

Fresh Tuna Burger with Mango Ketchup

Fresh tuna makes for a great burger. It has much of the consequence of a Classic Burger, but without as much fat. And after you taste it, mango ketchup may be the only ketchup you'll want to have.

BURGERS

1 pound ahi tuna, cut into 2-inch pieces

1 small onion, finely chopped

3 scallions, green parts only, finely chopped

¼ cup chopped fresh cilantro

2 tablespoons finely chopped garlic

2 tablespoons finely chopped peeled fresh ginger

1 tablespoon finely chopped jalapeño pepper

1 tablespoon Dijon mustard

1 teaspoon salt

Dash of hot sauce

MANGO KETCHUP

1 tablespoon vegetable oil

1 small onion, finely chopped

3 scallions, green parts only, coarsely chopped

2 tablespoons finely chopped peeled fresh ginger

1 tablespoon finely chopped garlic

1 ripe mango, peeled, pitted, and coarsely chopped

¼ cup chopped fresh cilantro

1 tablespoon finely chopped jalapeño pepper

2 tablespoons freshly squeezed lemon juice

1 teaspoon hot sauce made from Scotch bonnet peppers (see note, page 65)

½ teaspoon salt

½ cup flour for dredging

1 tablespoon salt

2 tablespoons vegetable oil

4 hamburger buns

To make the burgers: Combine all the burger ingredients in the bowl of a food processor fitted with a steel blade and pulse until finely chopped, about 6 pulses. Do not overprocess.

Shape the mixture into 4 burgers about ¾ inch thick and 4 inches across. Set these on a plate so they are not touching, cover well with plastic wrap, and refrigerate for at least 1 hour or up to 6 hours.

To make the Mango Ketchup: Place a medium sauté pan over medium-high heat and let it get hot, about 1 minute. Add the 1 tablespoon oil and spread it evenly over the pan. Add the onion, scallions, ginger, and garlic and cook, stirring often, until the onion begins to soften, about 3 minutes. Add the mango, cilantro, and jalapeño and cook 1 minute more. And the lemon juice, hot sauce, and ½ teaspoon salt and stir to combine.

Let the mixture cool slightly, then transfer to the bowl of a blender and pulse until just puréed, adding water 1 teaspoon at a time if necessary to facilitate blending. It should be the consistency of ketchup, but does not have to be perfectly smooth. Transfer to a serving bowl and set aside.

Combine the flour and 1 tablespoon salt in a large shallow bowl or pie plate and whisk together. Dredge the chilled tuna burgers in the flour so they are lightly dusted on both sides.

Place a skillet, preferably cast-iron, over medium-high heat, add the 2 tablespoons oil, and let it get hot, about 2 minutes. Arrange the burgers so they aren't touching and cook, uncovered, for 2 minutes. Turn and cook about 2 minutes more. The burgers should be rare to medium-rare.

Serve on the hamburger buns, topped with the Mango Ketchup.

MAKES 4 BURGERS

Note: An efficient way to dredge these is to lay the burgers one at a time in the pan of flour and sprinkle some flour over the top. With your fingers spread slightly, gently lift the burger and softly shake off the excess flour. It only needs to be lightly dusted. Dredge all the burgers before heating up the pan, otherwise the first one in will be done before the last is dusted with flour.

Note: These burgers are too delicate to cook on an outdoor grill.

Lobster Burger with Lime Dressing

This burger is luxurious, even indulgent. Man overboard! It's like the classic lobster roll shaped into a burger and then seared. It's not just an exceptional burger—it's exceptional food.

BURGERS

2 lobsters, 1½ pounds each

½ cup finely chopped celery

½ cup finely chopped onion

½ cup dried bread crumbs

¼ cup finely chopped red bell pepper

3 scallions, green parts only, finely chopped

2 tablespoons finely chopped garlic

2 tablespoons mayonnaise

1 large egg

LIME DRESSING

¼ cup mayonnaise

¼ cup reduced-fat sour cream

¼ cup freshly squeezed lime juice

1 tablespoon hot sauce made from Scotch bonnet peppers (see note, page 65)

1 tablespoon vegetable oil

1 tablespoon butter

4 hamburger buns

To make the burgers: In a large pot of boiling water, cook the lobsters for 8 minutes. Transfer to a large bowl and let them cool. Remove the meat from the tail and claws and chop into ½-inch pieces.

Place the lobster meat in a medium bowl. Add the remaining burger ingredients and mix until well combined. The mixture should be slightly moist.

Shape the mixture into 4 burgers about ¾ inch thick and 4 inches across. Arrange the burgers on a platter so they aren't touching, cover with plastic, and refrigerate for at least 1 hour and up to 6 hours.

To make the Lime Dressing: Mix all the dressing ingredients together in a small bowl. Cover with plastic wrap and refrigerate until ready to use.

Place a skillet, preferably cast-iron, over medium-high heat and add the oil and butter. Just when the butter stops sizzling, arrange the chilled burgers in the pan so they aren't touching and cook, uncovered, for 2 minutes, until a nice crust forms on the bottom. Turn carefully and cook about 2 minutes more.

Serve on the hamburger buns, topped with the Lime Dressing.

MAKES 4 BURGERS

Note: These burgers are too delicate to cook on an outdoor grill.

Old-Fashioned Crab Burger

Years ago, some nameless patrician chef liberated the Crab Burger from its proletarian bun and proceeded to serve them on a plate under the poncey moniker "Crab Cakes." Here, the crab cake has been stripped of pretense and restored to its true, original burger state.

CRAB BURGER SAUCE

6 tablespoons mayonnaise (reduced fat is fine)

1 tablespoon freshly squeezed lime juice

2 teaspoons Old Bay Seasoning

Several dashes of hot sauce

BURGERS

1 pound canned lump crabmeat, picked over to remove any cartilage or shell

¼ cup finely chopped pimentos

¼ cup finely chopped fresh Italian parsley

¼ cup mayonnaise (reduced fat is fine)

¼ cup plain dried bread crumbs

4 tablespoons finely chopped Canadian bacon (about 2 ounces)

3 scallions, green parts only, finely chopped

1 large egg

1½ teaspoons Old Bay Seasoning

1 teaspoon salt

Freshly ground pepper

2 tablespoons vegetable oil

4 hamburger buns

To make the Crab Burger Sauce: Mix all the sauce ingredients together in a small bowl and refrigerate until ready to serve.

To make the burgers: In a bowl, use your fingers to mix together all the burger ingredients including pepper to taste, being careful not to break up the lumps of crabmeat. Shape the mixture into 4 burgers about ¾ inch thick and 4 inches across. Cover with plastic and refrigerate for at least 1 hour and up to 6 hours.

Place a skillet, preferably cast-iron, over medium-high heat and let it get hot, about 2 minutes. Add the oil and spread it evenly over the pan. Arrange the burgers so they aren't touching and cook, uncovered, until they are nicely browned on the bottom, about 3 minutes. Turn and cook about 3 minutes more.

Serve on the hamburger buns, topped with a dollop of Crab Burger Sauce.

MAKES 4 BURGERS

Note: These burgers are too delicate to cook on an outdoor grill.

Portobello-Eggplant Burger with Smoked Mozzarella and Tapenade

This is not a burger in the sense that nothing is ground up and shaped into a patty, but this combo has a kind of burgerness about it. The meaty portobello enhanced by the smokiness of the mozzarella gives this vegetarian burger a hearty, almost carnivorous edge. You need a sturdy bun for this burger, like a semolina roll or some crusty French bread.

½ cup kalamata olives, pitted

2 anchovy fillets

1 teaspoon Dijon mustard

4 tablespoons olive oil

Four ½-inch-thick slices medium onion

Four ½-inch-thick slices peeled eggplant

4 portobello mushrooms, about 4 inches across, stemmed

Four ¼-inch-thick slices smoked mozzarella (see note)

4 semolina rolls or 4-inch lengths of crusty baguette

Four ½-inch-thick slices tomato

Combine the olives, anchovies, and mustard in a blender and process until just smooth. Set aside. (The tapenade will keep, covered and refrigerated, for up to 2 days.)

Place a skillet, preferably cast-iron, over medium-high heat and let it get hot, about 1 minute. Add 1 tablespoon of the olive oil and spread it evenly over the pan. Add the onion slices and cook 4 minutes, until lightly browned on the first side. Turn, taking care to keep the slices intact, and cook 4 minutes more to brown the second side. Transfer the onion slices to a platter and lay a piece of foil over them to keep them warm.

Add 1 more tablespoon of the olive oil and spread it evenly over the pan. Add the eggplant slices and cook 4 minutes, until they are lightly browned on the first side. Turn and cook 4 minutes more until softened and browned on the second side. Transfer the eggplant slices to the platter with the onions and re-cover to keep warm.

Add the remaining 2 tablespoons of the olive oil and spread it evenly over the pan. Add the mushrooms, top-side down, and cook 4 minutes, until they are lightly browned. Turn and place cheese slices on top of the mushrooms. Cook 4 minutes more. Transfer each mushroom to one of the rolls.

(continued)

Add the tomato slices to the pan and cook for 15 seconds. Turn and cook 15 seconds more. Remove and set aside.

Arrange an eggplant slice over the melted cheese on each of the mushrooms. Place an onion slice on the eggplant. Finish with a slice of tomato and serve topped with 2 tablespoons of the tapenade.

For charcoal-grilled burgers, make a medium fire (see note, page 12). Make sure the grate is clean and oiled. Brush the mushrooms, eggplant, and onion slices with oil and grill them all at the same time for 4 minutes. Turn and cook 4 to 5 minutes more. Place the slices of cheese on the mushrooms after turning. Serve the tomatoes on the sandwiches without grilling.

For gas-grilled burgers, preheat on medium-high until the grill is hot. Make sure the grate is clean and oiled. Brush the mushrooms, eggplant, and onion slices with oil and grill for 4 minutes with the cover closed. Turn and place the slices of cheese on the mushrooms. Cook 4 to 5 minutes more, cover closed. Serve the tomatoes on the sandwiches without grilling.

MAKES 4 BURGERS

Note: Smoked mozzarella is available in Italian markets and many specialty-food shops. If you can't find it, substitute smoked Cheddar. If you want to forgo the smoked cheese altogether, substitute plain mozzarella, Gorgonzola, Gruyère, or your favorite hard or semi-hard cheese.

SIDE DISHES

SOME PEOPLE HAVE A BURGER JUST TO HAVE SOMETHING to accompany their French fries. And, indeed, fries are Captain to the hamburg's Tenille. But the Rosemary Roasted Potatoes (page 80) will give the fries a run for their money, and the Curried Sweet Potatoes (page 84) could become your new reason to make a burger.

Most of these side dishes can be prepared ahead of time so you can totally focus on cooking the burgers. Potatoes should be kept warm in a low oven while you cook the burgers, and cold side dishes should be kept refrigerated until it's burger time.

Rosemary Roasted Potatoes

The distinctive, yet not overwhelming flavor of the rosemary in these potatoes will complement just about any of the burgers in this book.

2 pounds fingerling or small Yukon gold potatoes

3 tablespoons olive oil

1½ tablespoons fresh rosemary or 2 teaspoons dried

2 teaspoons salt

Freshly ground pepper

Preheat the oven to 375°F. Place the potatoes in a medium bowl. If any of the potatoes are particularly large, cut them in half. Add the olive oil, rosemary, salt, and pepper to taste and toss so all the potatoes are coated with oil.

Transfer to a 9-by-13-inch baking dish.

Bake, uncovered, on the center rack of the oven for about 50 minutes, or until the potatoes are tender. Serve immediately.

SERVES 4

Note: You can make the potatoes a few hours in advance and reheat in a 300°F oven for 10 minutes before serving, or serve them at room temperature. Either way, do not store them in a sealed container—they will get mealy. Leave them in the pan loosely covered with paper towels.

French Fries

Now that you're steadfastly making your own burgers, you have to make your own fries as well. And once you make them, you'll never want to eat any other fries but your own. You do need to invest in a candy thermometer, because this is the classic French method wherein the fries are cooked twice, with the oil at different temperatures. It's a small investment for something so sublime.

2½ pounds russet potatoes

4 cups vegetable oil

Salt

Wash and dry the potatoes. Fill a bowl with cold water and place it next to the cutting board. Cut the potatoes lengthwise, without peeling, into ½-inch slices. Then cut each slice into ½-inch strips. Place these immediately in the cold water to keep from browning. The water will also draw out some of the starch.

In a deep, heavy saucepan, heat the oil over medium-high heat. While the oil is heating, drain the potatoes and transfer to a baking sheet lined with paper towels. Pat the potatoes with more paper towels until they are completely dry. When the oil reaches 300°F, carefully drop a batch of fries, about 15, into the oil. Do not overcrowd. Cook for 2 minutes. The fries should still be white. Remove with a slotted spoon and transfer to another baking sheet lined with paper towels. Repeat with the remaining fries.

Let the fries come to room temperature. Reheat the oil to 375°F. Carefully drop the fries in batches in the oil and cook until they are golden brown, 2 to 3 minutes. Transfer to a baking sheet pan lined with clean, dry paper towels. Repeat until all the fries are cooked. Salt them to taste and serve immediately.

SERVES 4

Note: The fries can be cut and left soaking in the water early in the day, or even the night before. Just keep refrigerated until ready to use. The fries can also be cooked the first time up to 4 hours before being finished. Leave them at room temperature, covered with paper towels or a kitchen cloth. Do not cover with plastic.

Garlic Mashed Potatoes

Gimme *some* skin, but not a lot of skin, in my mashed potatoes. I peel off a wide ring of skin from the center of each spud before cooking. The potatoes are done when they are just tender. If you cook them too long, they turn into mush.

1 medium head garlic	1 tablespoon salt, plus 1 teaspoon
Olive oil for drizzling	¼ cup milk
2½ pounds Yukon gold potatoes	2 tablespoons butter

Preheat the oven to 375°F. Trim ½ inch off the wide (root) end of an unpeeled head of garlic. Drizzle some olive oil over the exposed cloves and place the head, cut-side down, on a square of aluminum foil. Wrap the garlic in the foil, and bake on the center rack of the oven until the garlic is soft, about 1 hour and 15 minutes. When cool enough to handle, squeeze the pulp out of the garlic skins into a small bowl and set aside.

With a peeler or paring knife, peel 2 to 3 inches of skin from around the center of each potato. Cut into large 2-inch pieces.

Place the potatoes in a medium pot, cover with cold water, and add the 1 tablespoon of salt. Bring to a boil over high heat, then reduce heat to a simmer. Cook until the potatoes are tender and the tip of a knife goes in easily but with a bit of resistance, about 14 minutes. Drain and transfer to a medium bowl.

During the last few minutes of cooking, heat the milk and butter in a small pan until the butter is melted.

Add the warmed milk and butter to the bowl with the potatoes, along with the roasted garlic pulp and the 1 teaspoon of salt. Mix together with a potato masher until just combined. Add more milk or salt if necessary. Serve immediately.

SERVES 4

Note: You may want to roast a few more heads of garlic at the same time to use for other dishes. They will last for 2 days, covered and refrigerated.

Curried Sweet Potatoes

Uncanny flavor with a simple preparation, these potatoes are particularly good with the Tandoori (page 36), Merguez (page 54), and Island Shrimp (page 62) burgers.

1 tablespoon olive oil

1 medium onion, halved lengthwise and cut into ¼-inch slices

¼ cup finely chopped garlic

¼ cup finely chopped peeled fresh ginger

3 tablespoons mild curry powder

1 teaspoon ground cumin

1 cup chicken broth

1 cup coconut milk

2 pounds sweet potatoes, peeled, halved lengthwise, and cut into ¼-inch slices

1 tart apple such as Granny Smith, peeled, quartered, and cut into ½-inch slices

Salt

Freshly ground pepper

Fresh chives or parsley for garnish

Place a large skillet over medium-high heat, add the oil, and let it get hot, about 1 minute. Add the onion slices and cook, stirring often, until they soften, about 5 minutes. Add the garlic and ginger and cook 1 minute more, stirring continuously. Add the curry powder and cumin and cook 30 seconds more, stirring continuously.

Add the broth and coconut milk and stir to combine. Add the sweet potato and apple slices and stir to coat them with the liquid.

Cover the pan, reduce the heat to low, and simmer for 20 minutes, stirring occasionally to keep the bottom from scorching.

Uncover and cook 5 minutes more, or until liquid has thickened and the potatoes are tender.

Transfer to a platter. Season with salt and pepper. Garnish with chopped chives or parsley and serve.

SERVES 4

Classic Cole Slaw

This old-fashioned slaw is the perfect accompaniment to a platter of burgers in the backyard on a summer afternoon or evening.

¼ cup mayonnaise

¼ cup sour cream

2 tablespoons white wine vinegar

1 tablespoon celery seeds

1 teaspoon sugar

1 teaspoon salt

2 cups shredded green cabbage

2 cups shredded red cabbage

1 cup grated carrot

½ cup thinly sliced red onion

In a small bowl, whisk together the mayonnaise, sour cream, vinegar, celery seeds, sugar, and salt until combined. Set aside.

In a large bowl, toss together the remaining ingredients. Add the dressing and toss to combine. Refrigerate until ready to serve.

SERVES 4

Fried Onion Rings

These are lighter than your usual bar-style onion rings, more like tempura. Using cake flour is an old trick that helps keep the batter light and the onion rings less soggy. It's important that the water and beer be very cold. Arrange the cooked onion rings on a baking sheet in a single layer, uncovered, when keeping them warm, otherwise they will lose their crispness. These go great with any of the Classic Burgers.

2 large Vidalia or other sweet onions, peeled

1½ cups cake flour

1 cup all-purpose flour

1 teaspoon cayenne pepper

1 teaspoon baking powder

2 egg whites

1½ cups very cold beer

1 cup very cold water

3 cups vegetable oil

Salt

Freshly ground pepper

Preheat the oven to 200°F.

Cut the onions into ⅓-inch slices and separate them into rings.

In a large bowl, whisk together the cake flour, all-purpose flour, cayenne, and baking powder until combined.

In a medium bowl, whisk the eggs whites until they are light and frothy, about 1 minute. Add the very cold beer and very cold water and whisk together quickly to combine. Add the beer mixture to the dry ingredients and whisk together until just combined. The batter will be loose and a little lumpy.

In a deep, heavy saucepan, heat the oil to 375°F.

Dip 3 onion rings into the batter and drop them carefully into the hot oil. Repeat quickly and carefully. Cook the 6 rings until they are golden brown, about 2 minutes.

Transfer with a slotted spoon to a baking sheet lined with paper towels and keep them warm in the oven until all the onion rings are cooked.

Season with salt and pepper and serve immediately.

SERVES 4

Note: If you can't find cake flour, increase the amount of all-purpose flour to 2 cups and add ½ cup cornstarch.

Herbed Red Potato Salad

Here's another backyard tradition that makes burgers taste even better. This is a basic creamy potato salad recipe. You may want to doctor it up the way your mother liked to do with, say, chopped hard-boiled eggs, capers, relish, chopped fennel, anchovies, or that secret ingredient she has kept to herself for so many years.

2 pounds small red potatoes	1 teaspoon Dijon mustard
1 tablespoon salt, plus 1 teaspoon	½ freshly ground pepper
¼ cup mayonnaise	½ cup diced red onion
¼ cup sour cream	½ cup diced celery
1 tablespoon finely chopped garlic	¼ cup julienned fresh basil

Place the potatoes in a medium pot, cover with cold water, and add the tablespoon of salt. Bring to a boil over high heat, then reduce the heat to a simmer. Cook until the potatoes are tender and the tip of a knife goes in easily but with a bit of resistance, about 14 minutes. Drain and cool.

In a medium bowl, whisk together the mayonnaise, sour cream, garlic, mustard, pepper, and the 1 teaspoon of salt. Set aside.

When the potatoes have cooled, cut them in half, leaving the skins on, and transfer to a medium bowl along with the onion, celery, and basil. Add the dressing and toss together.

Serve within the hour or refrigerate, letting it sit at room temperature 30 minutes before serving.

SERVES 4

Egg Cream

Cold beer, margueritas, a bottle of soda pop—each of these goes with some burgers, but only the diner-classic egg cream goes with almost any burger. It's the perfect drink to have with a mouthwatering burger and a big plate of fries—or it may be in its light but rich self the only side dish you need.

Milk

Chocolate syrup

Seltzer or sparkling water, chilled

Fill a large drinking glass one-fourth full of milk. Add 2 to 3 tablespoons of chocolate syrup and stir well. Slowly pour cold seltzer over the back of a spoon held inside the glass (to keep from fizzing over) until the glass is near full. Stir. The foam at the top (which looks like beaten egg whites) gives the drink its name.

   Drink.
   Repeat.

Note: Have plenty of ingredients on hand to serve your estimated number of thirsty guests.

Dessert Burger

Going all the way with the burger theme, this is the dream dessert after just about any burger course. Waffles and chocolate ice cream serve as the bun and burger, strawberry sauce as ketchup, whipped cream for the mayo, and kiwi slices for pickles.

4 ounces heavy or whipping cream or canned whipped cream

12 ounces frozen strawberries, thawed

2 teaspoons sugar

8 small frozen or homemade waffles (preferably round)

1 quart chocolate ice cream

2 kiwis, peeled and cut into ½-inch rounds

Whip the cream in a well-chilled medium bowl with beaters or a whisk until firm. Refrigerate until ready to use.

Place the strawberries and the sugar in a food processor fitted with a steel blade or blender and process until they are just puréed. It's okay if there are a few small pieces of berry left. Set aside.

Toast or make the waffles.

Scoop about 1 cup of the ice cream onto plastic wrap. Cover with another sheet of plastic wrap and roughly shape into a burger (don't knock yourself out—it's concept we're going for here, not verisimilitude).

Center the ice cream "burger" on 1 waffle. Cover with strawberry sauce. Top with some whipped cream. Cover with another waffle. Garnish with kiwi "pickles." Repeat with the remaining ingredients.

If you're making these for a crowd, assemble a perfect one for display; then you can be more cavalier preparing the others. They'll be eaten fast anyway—just like any other burger.

MAKES 4 "BURGERS"

INDEX

TABLE OF EQUIVALENTS

The exact equivalents in the following tables have been rounded for convenience.

LIQUID/DRY MEASURES

U.S.	METRIC
¼ teaspoon	1.25 milliliters
½ teaspoon	2.5 milliliters
1 teaspoon	5 milliliters
1 tablespoon (3 teaspoons)	15 milliliters
1 fluid ounce (2 tablespoons)	30 milliliters
¼ cup	60 milliliters
⅓ cup	80 milliliters
½ cup	120 milliliters
1 cup	240 milliliters
1 pint (2 cups)	480 milliliters
1 quart (4 cups, 32 ounces)	960 milliliters
1 gallon (4 quarts)	3.84 liters
1 ounce (by weight)	28 grams
1 pound	454 grams
2.2 pounds	1 kilogram

OVEN TEMPERATURE

FAHRENHEIT	CELSIUS	GAS
250	120	½
275	140	1
300	150	2
325	160	3
350	180	4
375	190	5
400	200	6
425	220	7
450	230	8
475	240	9
500	260	10

LENGTH

U.S.	METRIC
⅛ inch	3 millimeters
¼ inch	6 millimeters
½ inch	12 millimeters
1 inch	2.5 centimeters